MARTIN LUTHER KING JR.

By Barbara M. Linde

Gareth Stevens
Publishing

Please visit our website, www.garethstevens.com. For a free color catalog of all our high-quality books, call toll free 1-800-542-2595 or fax 1-877-542-2596.

Library of Congress Cataloging-in-Publication Data

Linde, Barbara M.
Martin Luther King Jr. / Barbara M. Linde.
    p. cm. — (Civil rights crusaders)
Includes index.
ISBN 978-1-4339-5692-8 (pbk.)
ISBN 978-1-4339-5693-5 (6-pack)
ISBN 978-1-4339-5690-4 (library binding)
1. King, Martin Luther, Jr., 1929-1968—Juvenile literature. 2. African Americans—Biography—Juvenile literature. 3. Civil rights workers—United States—Biography—Juvenile literature. 4. Baptists—United States—Clergy—Biography—Juvenile literature. 5. African Americans—Civil rights—History—20th century—Juvenile literature. I. Title.
E185.97.K5L53 2011
323.092—dc22
[B]
                                    2011002172

First Edition

Published in 2012 by
Gareth Stevens Publishing
111 East 14th Street, Suite 349
New York, NY 10003

Copyright © 2012 Gareth Stevens Publishing

Designer: Katelyn E. Reynolds
Editor: Kristen Rajczak

Photo credits: Cover, pp. 3–24, back cover (background) Shutterstock.com; cover, p. 1 Ernst Haas/Getty Images; pp. 5, 19 Robert Abbott Sengstacke/Getty Images; p. 7 New York Times Co./Getty Images; p. 9 Don Cravens/Time & Life Pictures/ Getty Images; p. 11 Paul Schutzer/Time & Life Pictures/Getty Images; p. 13 AFP/Getty Images; p. 15 Hulton Archive/Getty Images; p. 17 NY Daily News Archive via Getty Images.

Printed in the United States of America

CPSIA compliance information: Batch #CS11GS: For further information contact Gareth Stevens, New York, New York at 1-800-542-2595.

CONTENTS

Words in the glossary appear in **bold** type the first time they are used in the text.

CIVIL RIGHTS CRUSADER

Martin Luther King Jr. was an important **civil rights** leader. He wanted black Americans to have the same civil rights as white Americans. Martin fought against **discrimination** and **segregation**. He believed that all people were equal. Martin used peaceful actions to bring about change and told others to do the same. He once said, "There is nothing greater in all the world than freedom." Martin was murdered on April 4, 1968. His work and ideas live on today.

Martin speaks to a crowd in
Chicago, Illinois, in 1965.

5

EARLY LIFE

Martin Luther King Jr. was born on January 15, 1929, in Atlanta, Georgia. He went to segregated public schools. When Martin was 15 years old, he began attending Morehouse College. He finished in 1948. Martin became a Baptist **minister** that year, too. His father, grandfather, and great-grandfather were all Baptist ministers. After college, Martin continued his studies. He earned a **doctorate** in 1955.

Martin met Coretta Scott while they were both attending school in Boston, Massachusetts. They married in 1953. Later, they had four children.

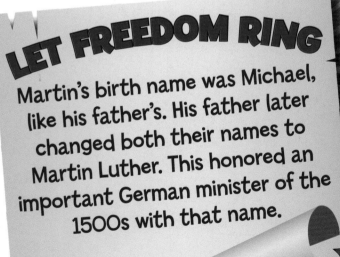

LET FREEDOM RING

Martin's birth name was Michael, like his father's. His father later changed both their names to Martin Luther. This honored an important German minister of the 1500s with that name.

Martin was a minister at Ebenezer Baptist Church in Atlanta, Georgia.

▽

7

THE MONTGOMERY BUS BOYCOTT

In 1955, even buses were segregated. Blacks had to ride in the back. On December 1, a black woman named Rosa Parks was on a bus in Montgomery, Alabama. When she refused to give her seat to a white man, she was arrested.

Groups that worked for racial equality organized a bus **boycott** in Montgomery. Martin helped lead the effort. For more than 380 days, civil rights supporters, both black and white, stopped using the buses. Finally, the US **Supreme Court** said segregated buses were illegal.

LET FREEDOM RING

Montgomery's law allowing segregation on buses was ruled unconstitutional. That means it went against the US Constitution.

This picture of Martin was taken in 1956 at the end of the bus boycott.

▽

PEACEFUL PROTESTS

Martin and other black ministers wanted to help organize and support civil rights **protests** in the South. Some blacks conducted "sit-ins" in restaurants. They sat until they were served. Others went on "freedom rides." They tested the Supreme Court's ruling on **integration** by riding buses throughout the South. The Southern Leadership Conference began in 1957 to aid these efforts. Martin was the president.

Martin was arrested many times for his role in the civil rights movement. However, he always tried to protest peacefully.

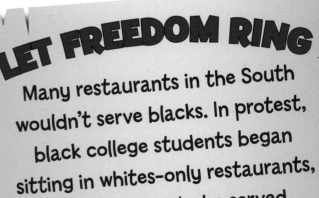

LET FREEDOM RING

Many restaurants in the South wouldn't serve blacks. In protest, black college students began sitting in whites-only restaurants, politely asking to be served.

Martin didn't support protests at which people used force or aimed to harm others.

▽

THE MARCH ON WASHINGTON

In 1963, segregation was still present in many places. Martin helped organize a march to support racial equality. On August 28, 1963, more than 200,000 people gathered in Washington, DC. The march was peaceful. The message was strong: Give black Americans their civil rights.

Martin gave a speech that became famous. He said, "I have a dream that one day . . . little black boys and black girls will be able to join hands with little white boys and white girls as sisters and brothers."

LET FREEDOM RING

The march was shown on television. Millions of viewers heard Martin's "I Have a Dream" speech.

Martin waves to the crowd at the March on Washington in 1963.

THE CIVIL RIGHTS AND VOTING ACTS

The government listened. The Civil Rights Act passed in 1964. This law made segregation and discrimination illegal.

Martin believed even more changes were needed. In 1965, he helped organize a march supporting black voting rights in Selma, Alabama. The police used force to stop the peaceful marchers. However, Martin wanted to make sure the marchers were heard. He organized two more marches.

The Voting Rights Act became a law in August 1965. People could no longer be stopped from voting because of their race or the color of their skin.

LET FREEDOM RING

Martin won the Nobel Peace Prize in 1964. He gave the $54,123 prize money to the civil rights movement.

President Lyndon B. Johnson invited Martin to see him sign the Civil Rights Act into law.

▽

Lyndon B. Johnson

△

15

CHANGES IN THE CIVIL RIGHTS MOVEMENT

Not all black Americans agreed with Martin's ideas about using peaceful actions to bring about change. By 1965, many people were following black **militants** like Malcolm X.

Martin always stayed true to his beliefs. He was against the war the United States was fighting in Vietnam. He thought the government should spend its money on helping poor Americans instead of war. He felt so strongly about it that he formed the Poor People's Campaign in 1967.

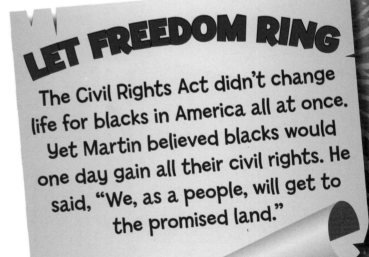

LET FREEDOM RING

The Civil Rights Act didn't change life for blacks in America all at once. Yet Martin believed blacks would one day gain all their civil rights. He said, "We, as a people, will get to the promised land."

Even when people didn't agree with him, Martin spoke about peace and equality.

THE ASSASSINATION

On April 4, 1968, Martin was **assassinated** in Memphis, Tennessee. His funeral took place on April 9 in Atlanta. His wife asked that a recording of Martin's last **sermon** be played. About 1,000 people filled Ebenezer Baptist Church. Another 50,000 or more people stood on the streets. Many people watched the funeral on television.

All over the country, people were both sad and angry. Schools and businesses closed. Groups had their own memorial services to remember him.

LET FREEDOM RING

Carved into Martin's gravestone are words from one of his famous speeches: "Free at last, free at last, thank God Almighty, I'm free at last."

Thousands of people paid their respects to Martin on the streets of Atlanta.

THE FIGHT CONTINUES

Martin Luther King Jr. gave his life to help the civil rights movement. People all over the United States still hear his message in their schools and communities.

Coretta Scott King started the King Center in 1968. Visitors to the King Center learn about Martin's life and work. In 1981, the center was moved to a building near Ebenezer Baptist Church. Coretta also asked the US government to recognize Martin's civil rights work. Since 1986, the nation has observed the third Monday in January as a holiday honoring Martin.

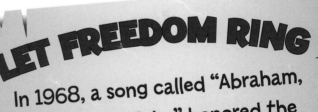

LET FREEDOM RING

In 1968, a song called "Abraham, Martin, and John" honored the civil rights work of Abraham Lincoln, Martin Luther King Jr., and John F. Kennedy.

TIMELINE

1929   Martin Luther King Jr. is born on January 15.

1948   Martin becomes a Baptist minister.

1953   Martin marries Coretta Scott.

1955   Martin earns a doctorate.

1957   Martin helps start the Southern Christian Leadership Conference.

1963   Martin leads marches in Alabama and Washington, DC.

1964   The Civil Rights Act passes. Martin wins the Nobel Peace Prize.

1965   The Voting Rights Act passes.

1968   Martin is killed on April 4 in Memphis, Tennessee. The King Center opens.

1986   Martin Luther King Jr. Day becomes a national holiday.

GLOSSARY

assassinate: to kill someone, especially a public figure

boycott: the act of refusing to have dealings with a person or business in order to force change

civil rights: the freedoms granted to us by law

discrimination: treating people differently because of their race or beliefs

doctorate: the highest degree given by a university. It requires many years of study.

integration: the process of making a place or organization open to all races

militant: a person who will use force to support a cause or beliefs

minister: a person who leads a church service

protest: an event at which a group objects to an idea, an act, or a way of doing something

segregation: the forced separation of races or classes

sermon: a speech given at a church service, which provides a lesson

Supreme Court: the highest court in the United States

FOR MORE INFORMATION

Books

McWhorter, Diane. *A Dream of Freedom: The Civil Rights Movement from 1954 to 1968*. New York, NY: Scholastic, 2004.

Pastan, Amy. *Martin Luther King, Jr.* New York, NY: DK Publishing, 2004.

Rappaport, Doreen. *Martin's Big Words: The Life of Dr. Martin Luther King, Jr.* New York, NY: Hyperion Paperbacks for Children, 2007.

Websites

Dr. Martin Luther King, Jr.
www.naacp.org/pages/king
Learn more about the history of the organization as well as Martin's work.

The King Center
www.thekingcenter.org
Watch videos and hear Martin's speeches.

The Martin Luther King, Jr., National Historic Site
www.nps.gov/nr/travel/atlanta/kin.htm
See the neighborhood in Atlanta, Georgia, where Martin lived and went to school.

INDEX